FACTS AND FIGURES ABOUT SWITZERLAND DEROUSEY SCHOOL

A Compelling and Prospectus Guide of the most Expensive School in the World.

David Scott

TABLE OF CONTENTS

INTRODUCTION

LeRosey School, also known as the Institute Le Rosey, is a private boarding school in Rolle, Switzerland. Founded in 1880, it is one of the oldest and most prestigious boarding schools in the world, known for its academic excellence, rich history, and breathtaking campus. Here are some facts and figures about Le RoseyLe Rosey School:

The School was founded by Paul Carnal as a boys' boarding school. It was the first school in Switzerland to combine academic excellence with outdoor activities such as skiing, sailing, and horse riding.

The campus of Le RoseyLe Rosey School is spread over 28 hectares and includes two campuses, one in Rolle and one in Gstaad. The campus features state-of-the-art facilities, including modern classrooms, sports fields, music rooms, a theater, and an art gallery.

Le RoseyLe Rosey School is a co-educational school with around 400 students aged between 8 and 18 from over 60 countries. The school has a diverse student body with a mix of nationalities, cultures, and languages.

Also and very more professionally, the School offers a bilingual education in French and English, with a strong emphasis on academic excellence, creativity, and personal development. The school follows the International Baccalaureate (IB) program, which prepares students for admission to top universities around the world.

Unlike many conventional schools, Le RoseyLe Rosey offers a wide range of extracurricular activities, including sports, music, art, theater, and community service.

The school has a strong tradition of outdoor education, with activities such as skiing, sailing, and hiking.

Le Rosey School has a prestigious list of alumni, including members of royalty, politicians, artists, and business leaders. Some notable alumni include Prince Rainier III of Monaco, Shah Mohammad Reza Pahlavi of Iran, and fashion designer Hubert de Givenchy.

Le Rosey School is one of the oldest and most prestigious boarding schools in the world, known for its academic excellence, diverse student body, and stunning campus. With its bilingual education, extracurricular activities, and strong emphasis on personal development, Le RoseyLe Rosey School prepares students for success in the global community.

The Le Rosey School is an incredible institution that has been educating students for over 160 years. Founded in 1880 by Paul-Emile Carnal, Le Rosey has become a world-renowned school and one of the most prestigious private schools in Switzerland. Each year, the school's 600 students come from around the globe to experience the unique educational offerings of Le Rosey. The school's curriculum is highly diverse and includes everything from classes in the humanities to courses in the sciences and mathematics. Le Rosey also offers its students a wide range of extracurricular activities, such as sports, music, and art. It is no wonder why so many families from all over the world choose Le Rosey for their children's education. Le Rosey is a place of learning, creativity, and joy.

Over the years, Le Rosey has grown in size and reputation, becoming one of the most famous and exclusive schools in the world.
The school has a long and fascinating history. Here are some key events and milestones:

In 1911, Le Rosey moved to its current location in Rolle, overlooking Lake Geneva.

During World War II, the school temporarily moved to Lugano in southern Switzerland to avoid the conflict.

Le Rosey became a co-educational school in 1967, admitting girls for the first time.

The school has a long list of notable alumni, including kings, politicians, business leaders, and celebrities. Some of the most famous graduates include Prince Rainier III of Monaco, King Albert II of Belgium, John Kerry, and Sir Roger Moore.

In addition to its main campus in Rolle, Le Rosey also operates a winter campus in the Swiss Alps and a summer campus in Gstaad.

The school has a reputation for academic excellence, offering a rigorous curriculum that includes language learning, humanities, and STEM subjects. Students also have access to a wide range of extracurricular activities, such as sports, music, drama, and community service.

Le Rosey is known for its strict dress code, which requires students to wear a uniform of tailored jackets, ties, and kilts or skirts. This dress code is intended to promote a sense of discipline, tradition, and unity among students.

Today, Le Rosey remains one of the most prestigious and exclusive schools in the world, attracting students from around the globe who are seeking a world-class education and a unique cultural experience.With a student body that includes royalty, celebrities, and business leaders, Le Rosey School is often shrouded in mystique and intrigue. In this article, we will delve into the facts about Le Rosey School, exploring its fascinating history, notable alumni, and what makes it one of the most sought-after schools in the world.

Le Rosey School has become synonymous with academic excellence, cultural diversity, and unparalleled opportunities for students. In this article, we will explore some of the most fascinating facts about Le Rosey School, from its famous alumni to its unique traditions and distinctive curriculum. Whether you are a current or prospective student, or simply interested in learning more about this iconic institution, read on to discover some of the incredible facts about Le Rosey School.

CHAPTER ONE □
History and Objectives of Its Establishment

Founded in 1880 by Paul-Emile Carnal in the cite of the 14th century Chateau du Rosey in the town of Rolle in the canton of Vaud, it is among the oldest boarding school in Switzerland and one of the most prestigious and expensive schools in the world, for which is known as the"School of Kings"

Le Rosey School, founded in 1880, holds a distinguished place in the annals of education. With a rich heritage spanning over a century, Le Rosey has stood as a symbol of excellence, innovation, and global diversity. From its humble beginnings as a small boarding school nestled in the Swiss Alps to its current status as an internationally acclaimed institution, Le

Rosey has consistently pursued a set of unwavering objectives.

First and foremost, Le Rosey strives to provide an unparalleled educational experience. The school's commitment to academic rigor, intellectual curiosity, and critical thinking ensures that students receive a world-class education. Through a comprehensive curriculum that embraces both traditional subjects and contemporary disciplines, Le Rosey equips students with the knowledge and skills necessary to excel in an ever-changing world.

Beyond academic excellence, Le Rosey places a strong emphasis on the development of character and personal growth. The school fosters an inclusive and supportive environment, encouraging students to explore their passions, take risks, and embrace challenges. Le Rosey recognizes that education extends beyond the classroom walls, and thus offers a wide range of extracurricular activities, including sports, arts, and community service, enabling students to discover their talents, build resilience, and cultivate a well-rounded personality.

One of the defining features of Le Rosey is its commitment to internationalism. As one of the first truly international boarding schools, Le Rosey has a long-standing tradition of welcoming students from all corners of the globe. By fostering a multicultural community, the school promotes intercultural understanding, empathy, and global citizenship. Through daily interactions and collaborative projects, students learn to appreciate diversity, develop cross-cultural competencies, and become compassionate global leaders.

Le Rosey's objectives extend beyond the individual student to a broader vision of creating positive change in the world. The school instills a sense of social responsibility and environmental stewardship in its students. By integrating sustainable practices into its operations and curriculum, Le Rosey empowers students to address pressing global issues, such as climate change, inequality, and social injustice. The school's commitment to service learning and philanthropy further encourages students to make a meaningful impact on society.

For all ramifications, Le RoseyLe Rosey School stands as a testament to the power of education and its ability to shape young minds and transform lives. With a rich history and a clear set of objectives, Le Rosey continues to inspire generations of students to embrace knowledge, seek excellence, and become compassionate leaders in an increasingly interconnected world.

Achievable Objectives by Curriculum and Extracurricular Activities

Le Rosey School has successfully achieved its objectives through a combination of a robust curriculum and a wide range of extracurricular activities, as evidenced by the following statistics:

1. Academic Excellence:

Graduates of Le Rosey consistently achieve exceptional academic results.
The school boasts a high percentage of students who gain admission to prestigious universities and colleges worldwide.
Le Rosey alumni have gone on to pursue successful careers in various fields, further demonstrating the effectiveness of the curriculum.

2. **Comprehensive Curriculum:**

Le Rosey's curriculum encompasses a diverse range of subjects, including sciences, humanities, languages, and the arts.

The school offers Advanced Placement (AP) courses and International Baccalaureate (IB) programs, providing students with rigorous academic challenges and opportunities for advanced learning.

The curriculum is designed to foster critical thinking, problem-solving skills, and a deep understanding of complex concepts.

Multidisciplinary Approach:

Le Rosey encourages interdisciplinary learning, allowing students to make connections between different subjects and explore the intersections of knowledge.

The school promotes an inquiry-based learning approach, where students actively engage in research, analysis, and independent thinking.

The school's educational approach and emphasis on critical thinking suggest the development of strong problem-solving abilities.

Here are key aspects that contribute to the cultivation of problem-solving skills at Le Rosey:

Inquiry-Based Learning: Le Rosey promotes an inquiry-based learning approach, where students are encouraged to ask questions, investigate problems, and seek creative solutions. This method stimulates critical thinking, problem-solving, and independent learning.

Interdisciplinary Education: Le Rosey's curriculum integrates various disciplines, allowing students to make connections between subjects and apply knowledge to real-world situations. This interdisciplinary approach nurtures analytical thinking and problem-solving abilities across different contexts.

Collaborative Projects: Le Rosey emphasizes collaborative learning experiences, including group projects and teamwork. By working together on complex tasks, students develop problem-solving skills, effective communication, and the ability to negotiate and compromise.

Case Studies and Simulations: Le Rosey incorporates case studies and simulations into the learning process, providing students with opportunities to analyze and solve realistic problems. These exercises encourage critical thinking, decision-making, and the application of knowledge in practical scenarios.

Advanced Programs: Le Rosey offers Advanced Placement (AP) courses and International Baccalaureate (IB) programs, which emphasize higher-order thinking skills and problem-solving abilities. Students engage with challenging coursework that encourages analysis, evaluation, and innovative solutions.

Extracurricular Activities: Participation in extracurricular activities, such as debate clubs, robotics teams, and science fairs, allows students to tackle complex challenges and find creative solutions. These experiences foster problem-solving skills, adaptability, and resilience.

Individualized Support: Le Rosey provides individualized attention and support to students, enabling them to identify and overcome obstacles. Through personalized guidance from teachers and mentors, students develop problem-solving strategies tailored to their unique strengths and weaknesses.

Although concrete statistics on problem-solving skills may not be available, the educational philosophy and practices at Le

Rosey School align with the cultivation of these crucial abilities.

The school's emphasis on critical thinking, interdisciplinary education, collaborative projects, and practical applications empowers students to become proficient problem solvers, equipping them with the skills needed to navigate challenges and make positive contributions in the world.

By integrating technology and innovation into the curriculum, Le Rosey equips students with the necessary skills for the digital age.

Extracurricular Activities:

Le Rosey School is renowned for its extracurricular activities. Statistics show that over 75% of Le Rosey students are involved in some sort of extra-curricular activity. Of this 75%, 24% are involved in sports, 18% in music, 17% in theater, 14% in debate, and 12% in other extracurricular activities.

Sports are a huge part of the Le Rosey culture, with over 25 different sports, ranging from lacrosse, hockey, and squash, to golf and cricket. Music is also very popular at Le Rosey, with a number of different groups and activities available to students. Theater is a big part of the school's culture, with a number of plays and musicals performed by students and faculty each year. Debate is also popular at Le Rosey, with an active debate team and a number of different clubs available to students.

In addition to these activities, Le Rosey also offers a number of other extracurricular activities, such as clubs, community service projects, and volunteer work. These activities provide important learning opportunities for students, as well as a chance to meet new people and explore new interests.

Overall, Le Rosey provides its students with a wide variety of extracurricular activities to choose from. The statistics show that the school's extracurricular activities are an integral part of the student experience and are a major factor in why Le Rosey is such a successful and popular school.

The school has state-of-the-art facilities and dedicated coaches and instructors, enabling students to excel in their chosen fields.

Through participation in extracurricular activities, students develop leadership skills, teamwork, time management, and a sense of discipline.

● Global Diversity and Cultural Exchange

Le Rosey's commitment to internationalism is reflected in its student body, comprising students from different countries and cultural backgrounds.

The school promotes cultural exchange through activities such as international festivals, language clubs, and exchange programs with partner schools worldwide.

The diverse student population fosters a global perspective, empathy, and intercultural understanding.

Recognition and Accreditations:

Le Rosey has earned prestigious accreditations and memberships, demonstrating its commitment to high educational standards. These include accreditations from organizations such as the International Baccalaureate (IB) and the Council of International Schools (CIS).

The school's reputation as a leading educational institution has garnered recognition and respect from universities, employers, and educational authorities worldwide.

By combining a rigorous curriculum with a diverse range of extracurricular activities, Le Rosey School has consistently achieved its objectives of academic excellence, holistic development, and global citizenship. The statistics highlight the effectiveness of these approaches in shaping well-rounded individuals prepared for success in higher education and beyond.

The following are general understanding of the diversity and cultural values commonly associated with the institution. Please note that specific statistics may vary from year to year.

International Student Body: Le Rosey attracts students from diverse nationalities, offering a global representation within its student body. It is known for having a significant number of students from various countries, contributing to its multicultural environment.

Language Diversity: The school promotes multilingualism and encourages students to learn multiple languages. Students at Le Rosey typically have the opportunity to study and communicate in different languages, further enhancing their cultural understanding and language skills.

Cultural Celebrations: Le Rosey values cultural celebrations and encourages students to share and celebrate their unique traditions. The school may organize events and activities that showcase the cultural diversity of its student body, fostering an inclusive and festive atmosphere.

Exchange Programs: Le Rosey may have partnerships with other schools or organizations worldwide, facilitating student exchanges. These programs allow students to experience different cultures firsthand, promoting intercultural dialogue and understanding.

Cultural Studies: The curriculum at Le Rosey often includes courses or activities that explore global cultures, histories, and art forms. Students have the opportunity to learn about various cultural perspectives, promoting tolerance and appreciation for diversity.

Respect and Inclusion: Le Rosey emphasizes respect for individual differences and fosters an inclusive environment. The school encourages students to embrace diversity, cultivating an atmosphere of acceptance and understanding.

It's important to note that Le Rosey's commitment to diversity and cultural values may evolve over time, and the specific statistics and initiatives may vary. For the most accurate and up-to-date information, I recommend visiting Le Rosey's official website or contacting the school directly.

CHAPTER TWO □

Archi-Technical Structure of The Sectional Edification

The sectional edification of Le Rosey School is characterized by a carefully designed architectural structure that maximizes functionality, aesthetics, and the overall student experience. This detailed exploration highlights the key elements of the school's sectional edification.

The primary building complex, Château du Rosey, serves as the centerpiece of the school's sectional edification. This grand structure showcases a multi-level design that accommodates various educational and administrative functions. The ground floor typically houses common areas such as reception areas, administrative offices, and communal spaces. These spaces are strategically positioned to facilitate easy access for students, faculty, and visitors, promoting efficient circulation and a welcoming atmosphere.

Moving upward, the upper floors of Château du Rosey house classrooms, lecture halls, and specialized learning spaces. These levels are meticulously organized to ensure a logical and efficient flow between different academic departments. The placement of classrooms takes into account factors such as natural lighting, views, and noise control, optimizing the learning environment for students.

Adjacent to Château du Rosey are the residential buildings, which form an integral part of the sectional edification. These structures provide dormitories and housing for students and staff, creating a sense of community and fostering a supportive living environment. The residential buildings are often designed with multiple floors, accommodating individual rooms or suites that offer privacy while also encouraging social interaction through shared spaces such as lounges, study areas, and common rooms.

In addition to the primary buildings, the sectional edification of Le Rosey School incorporates recreational and athletic facilities. These structures are often designed with large open spaces and multiple levels to accommodate a variety of sporting activities, including gyms, swimming pools, tennis courts, and playing fields. The placement of these facilities within the sectional edification encourages a healthy and active lifestyle, while also providing opportunities for socialization, teamwork, and personal growth.

Throughout the sectional edification of Le Rosey School, careful attention is given to the integration of natural elements and the surrounding landscape. The buildings are designed to take advantage of natural lighting and ventilation, reducing energy consumption and creating a pleasant indoor environment. Outdoor spaces such as courtyards, gardens, and terraces are seamlessly incorporated, offering students and faculty opportunities for relaxation, recreation, and connection with nature.

Moreover, the sectional edification of Le Rosey School prioritizes accessibility and inclusivity. Consideration is given to the design of ramps, elevators, and other accommodations to ensure that individuals with mobility challenges can navigate the campus comfortably. This commitment to accessibility reinforces the school's inclusive philosophy, fostering a supportive and equitable learning environment for all.

Thus, the sectional edification of Le Rosey School embodies a thoughtful and purposeful approach to architectural design. The integration of different buildings, the optimization of space and functionality, the incorporation of natural elements, and the prioritization of accessibility all contribute to an enriching and inspiring environment for students, faculty, and staff. This detailed architectural structure not only supports the educational mission of the school but also reflects its commitment to excellence, innovation, and the holistic development of its community.

Le Rosey School exhibits several notable architectural patterns that contribute to its unique and powerful identity. These patterns not only enhance the functionality of the school but also encapsulate its rich history and educational philosophy.

First and foremost, Le Rosey School embraces a blend of architectural styles that harmoniously coexist within its campus. The school's main building, Château du Rosey, showcases a classic architectural pattern with its elegant façade, symmetrical design, and ornate detailing. This pattern evokes a sense of grandeur and tradition, reflecting the school's prestigious heritage.

In contrast, the surrounding buildings display a more modern architectural pattern, characterized by clean lines, large windows, and an emphasis on simplicity and functionality. This juxtaposition of styles creates a dynamic and visually captivating environment, symbolizing the school's commitment to both preserving tradition and embracing innovation.

Furthermore, the campus layout at Le Rosey School incorporates a deliberate pattern of interconnected spaces that foster a sense of community and collaboration. The arrangement of classrooms, residential buildings, recreational areas, and common spaces encourages interaction and cross-pollination among students, faculty, and staff. This architectural pattern promotes social engagement, dialogue, and the exchange of ideas, which are fundamental aspects of the school's educational philosophy.

Another striking architectural pattern at Le Rosey School is the integration of natural elements and the surrounding landscape. The campus is situated in a picturesque setting, nestled amidst rolling hills, lush gardens, and serene lakes. The buildings are strategically positioned to take full advantage of the stunning views and to seamlessly blend with the natural environment. This pattern creates a harmonious relationship between the built and natural spaces, fostering a sense of tranquility, inspiration, and connection with nature.

Lastly, the architectural patterns of Le Rosey School reflect its commitment to sustainability and environmental consciousness. The campus incorporates innovative design features, such as energy-efficient systems, renewable energy sources, and eco-friendly materials. This pattern aligns with the school's emphasis on global citizenship and responsible stewardship of the environment, imparting important values to the students.

In reality, the architectural patterns of Le Rosey School are a testament to its rich heritage, educational philosophy, and commitment to excellence. The blend of classic and modern styles, interconnected spaces, integration with nature, and sustainable design principles all contribute to the school's unique and powerful identity. Le Rosey School's architecture goes beyond aesthetics, creating an environment that inspires and nurtures its students, faculty, and community.

The architectural patterns observed in Le Rosey School encompass a fascinating subject of scientific inquiry, revealing insights into the design principles, historical context, and educational philosophy of the institution. This scientific introduction aims to explore and analyze these architectural patterns, shedding light on their significance and the impact they have on the school environment.

Architecture, as an interdisciplinary field, combines elements of engineering, aesthetics, sociology, and psychology to create built environments that are both functional and meaningful. Le Rosey School, renowned for its prestigious educational offerings, exhibits a rich tapestry of architectural patterns that contribute to the school's unique identity and educational mission.

By examining the architectural patterns employed within Le Rosey School, we can unravel the historical context that shapes the institution's design choices. The main building, Château du Rosey, embodies a classic architectural pattern, featuring an elegant façade, symmetrical design, and intricate detailing. These patterns are reminiscent of the historical and cultural influences that have shaped the school over time, reflecting its prestigious heritage.

In addition to historical influences, the architectural patterns of Le Rosey School also reflect the institution's forward-thinking approach to education. The incorporation of modern architectural patterns, characterized by clean lines, spacious interiors, and an emphasis on functionality, exemplifies the school's commitment to innovation and contemporary pedagogical practices. These patterns create an environment that is conducive to learning, collaboration, and adaptability, aligning with the school's educational philosophy.

Furthermore, the layout and spatial organization of Le Rosey School exhibit an architectural pattern that fosters community engagement and social interaction.

The interconnected spaces, strategically arranged classrooms, residential buildings, and common areas encourage the exchange of ideas and nurture a sense of belonging among students, faculty, and staff. This pattern of spatial connectivity promotes social integration, collaboration, and holistic development, fundamental aspects of the school's educational mission.

The integration of natural elements within the architectural patterns of Le Rosey School is another intriguing area of scientific exploration. The campus, set amidst breathtaking landscapes of rolling hills, vibrant gardens, and serene lakes, incorporates natural elements to enhance the overall ambiance and connection with the surrounding environment. This integration not only promotes a sense of harmony between the built and natural spaces but also provides opportunities for outdoor learning, recreation, and environmental stewardship.

Finally, the architectural patterns of Le Rosey School intersect with the principles of sustainability and environmental consciousness. The incorporation of energy-efficient systems, renewable energy sources, and eco-friendly materials within the design exemplify the school's commitment to sustainability and responsible environmental practices. Scientific analysis of these patterns can shed light on the effective integration of sustainability measures into architectural design and the impact they have on the school's ecological footprint.

Therefore, the architectural patterns of Le Rosey School present an intriguing subject of scientific investigation, encompassing historical, educational, sociological, and environmental aspects. Understanding these patterns provides valuable insights into the design principles and philosophy of the school, contributing to a broader understanding of the relationship between architecture and education. By examining the architectural patterns at Le Rosey School through a scientific lens, we can gain a deeper appreciation for the profound influence of the built environment on teaching, learning, and the overall student experience.

Le Rosey School encompasses various important designs, buildings, and departments that contribute to its functioning and character.

• The Main Building - Château du Rosey

Château du Rosey: The main building of Le Rosey School, Château du Rosey, is a prominent architectural feature. It houses administrative offices, classrooms, lecture halls, and communal spaces.

The main building of Le Rosey School, Château du Rosey, serves as the heart and symbol of the institution. Here are some highlights and statistics that reflect the purpose and significance of this iconic structure:

Historical Significance: Château du Rosey, dating back to the 14th century, holds immense historical and architectural significance. Its rich heritage and timeless charm create an inspiring and unique learning environment for students.

● Facts and figures

Beautiful Setting: Nestled amidst the stunning Swiss countryside in Rolle, Château du Rosey provides a picturesque backdrop for academic pursuits and student life. Its serene and scenic surroundings contribute to a tranquil and conducive atmosphere for learning.

Size and Scope: The main building spans a substantial area, with extensive facilities and spaces dedicated to various academic, artistic, and recreational activities. Its grandeur and scale reflect the school's commitment to providing a comprehensive and holistic educational experience.

Classrooms and Lecture Halls: Château du Rosey houses spacious classrooms and lecture halls equipped with modern amenities and technology. These spaces are designed to facilitate interactive and engaging teaching methods, fostering a dynamic learning environment.

Administrative Offices: Within the main building, administrative offices cater to the needs of students, faculty, and staff. These offices provide support and guidance, ensuring the smooth operation of the school and addressing the various administrative aspects of student life.

Dormitories: Château du Rosey accommodates student dormitories, offering a comfortable and nurturing home away from home for students. The dormitories are designed to provide a safe and supportive living environment, fostering a sense of community and camaraderie among the student body.

Cultural and Performance Spaces: The main building boasts spaces dedicated to the arts, including theaters, music rooms, and exhibition areas. These venues serve as platforms for students to showcase their talents, express their creativity, and engage in cultural activities.

Dining Facilities: Château du Rosey features dining halls and cafeterias that cater to the nutritional needs of students, offering a diverse and balanced menu. These communal spaces foster social interactions and provide opportunities for students to bond over meals.

Château du Rosey, as the main building of Le Rosey School, embodies the school's commitment to providing a world-class education in a nurturing and inspiring environment. Its historical significance, expansive facilities, and beautiful surroundings create a distinctive setting for students to thrive academically, artistically, and personally.

Residential Buildings: Le Rosey School has several residential buildings to accommodate students and staff. These buildings provide dormitories and housing facilities, creating a vibrant and supportive community atmosphere.

Sciences Building: Le Rosey School emphasizes the importance of scientific education, and thus has a dedicated Sciences Building. This facility is equipped with state-of-the-art laboratories and resources for conducting various scientific experiments and research.

Arts Center: Recognizing the significance of arts education, Le Rosey School boasts an Arts Center that includes studios, exhibition spaces, and specialized facilities for students interested in visual arts, music, and drama.

Sports Facilities: The school's campus includes extensive sports facilities to promote physical fitness and athletic development. These facilities may include sports halls, swimming pools, tennis courts, and playing fields.

Music Conservatory: Le Rosey School places a strong emphasis on music education, and thus has a music conservatory where students can pursue their musical talents. The conservatory may house practice rooms, music studios, and performance spaces.

Language Departments: Given the school's international character, Le Rosey School typically has language departments that offer instruction in multiple languages. These departments may have dedicated classrooms and language laboratories to facilitate language learning.

Library and Media Center: Le Rosey School recognizes the importance of research and academic resources, and therefore has a well-equipped library and media center. This space provides access to a wide range of books, digital resources, and study areas for students and faculty.

Dining Halls: Le Rosey School provides dining facilities where students and staff can gather for meals. These dining halls are designed to accommodate the school's population and offer a variety of food options.

CHAPTER THREE ☐
Guide To A Prospectus Applicants

Welcome to Le Rosey School, where dreams are nurtured, potential is unleashed, and futures are transformed. As you hold this prospectus in your hands, you stand at the threshold of an extraordinary educational journey, one that promises to shape your path and illuminate your potential like no other.

Le Rosey School is not merely a place of learning; it is a gateway to a world of endless possibilities, where academic excellence, cultural diversity, and personal growth converge to create an unparalleled educational experience. As you embark on this remarkable adventure, prepare to be inspired, challenged, and empowered to become the best version of yourself.

The keys to your future await you at La Rosey School. Are you ready to unlock them?
Welcome to the comprehensive Guide to Le Rosey School, crafted exclusively for our esteemed prospectus applicants. Within these pages, you will discover the essence of our institution, our educational philosophy, and the myriad opportunities that await you.

Le Rosey School is more than just an educational institution; it is a vibrant and close-knit community that fosters academic excellence, personal growth, and global citizenship. Our commitment to holistic education is at the core of everything we do. From our esteemed faculty to our state-of-the-art facilities, every aspect of Le Rosey is designed to empower and inspire our students.

As you peruse this guide, you will delve into the unique features that set Le Rosey apart. Our rigorous academic curriculum, shaped by our world-class educators, stimulates intellectual curiosity and prepares students for success in an ever-evolving world. With a focus on critical thinking, creativity, and interdisciplinary learning, our students are equipped with the skills necessary to navigate the challenges of the 21st century.

Beyond academics, Le Rosey embraces the arts, sports, and cultural enrichment as integral components of a well-rounded education. Our robust extracurricular program offers a plethora of opportunities for students to explore their passions, develop their talents, and cultivate a sense of camaraderie. From performing on our grand stage to competing in international sports tournaments, Le Rosey students are encouraged to embrace their unique abilities and strive for excellence in all endeavors.

At Le Rosey, cultural diversity is celebrated and cherished. Our international community, comprised of students from over 80 nations, provides a rich tapestry of perspectives and experiences that enhances global awareness and understanding. The connections forged at Le Rosey extend far beyond the school years, creating a lifelong network of friendships and professional relationships that span the globe.

While our commitment to academic rigor and personal growth is unwavering, we also place great emphasis on nurturing individual well-being. Le Rosey's supportive and inclusive environment ensures that each student feels valued and empowered to thrive. Our dedicated staff and comprehensive student support services are readily available to provide guidance and care, ensuring that every student's unique needs are met.

As you embark on your journey with Le Rosey, we encourage you to envision the limitless possibilities that lie ahead. Whether you aspire to become a leader in your chosen field, a global ambassador, or a catalyst for positive change, La Rosey will provide the foundation upon which your dreams can flourish.

We invite you to immerse yourself in the pages of this guide, to explore the diverse opportunities that await you at Le Rosey School. Prepare to embark on an educational odyssey that will shape your future, ignite your passions, and transform your life. Welcome to Le Rosey, where excellence knows no boundaries.

• Bounds and Out of Bounds For The Prospectus Applicants

Prospectus applicants of Le Rosey School should familiarize themselves with the bounds and out of bounds, which outline the guidelines and expectations for their application process. Understanding these boundaries will help ensure a smooth and respectful engagement with the school.

Here are some key points to consider:

Bounds

Authenticity: Applicants are expected to provide accurate and truthful information throughout the application process. Falsifying or misrepresenting information is strictly prohibited.

Respectful Communication: All interactions with Le Rosey School, including written correspondence, interviews, and campus visits, should be conducted in a polite and respectful manner. It is important to treat all staff, faculty, and fellow applicants with courtesy and professionalism.

Timeliness: Applicants are encouraged to adhere to deadlines and submit their application materials within the specified timeframes. Prompt and timely communication is appreciated.

Confidentiality: Any confidential or sensitive information shared during the application process should be handled with utmost discretion and not disclosed to unauthorized individuals or third parties.
Out of Bounds:

Plagiarism: Applicants must avoid any form of plagiarism in their application materials. This includes copying or using someone else's work, ideas, or statements without proper attribution.

Disruptive Behavior: Any behavior that disrupts the application process, such as harassment, intimidation, or disrespectful conduct towards school representatives or fellow applicants, is strictly prohibited.

Unauthorized Assistance: Applicants should complete their application materials independently and without unauthorized assistance. This includes written essays, personal statements, and any other components of the application.

Non-Compliance with Guidelines: Failure to follow the provided guidelines for application submission, such as document formatting requirements or specific instructions, may result in disqualification or delays in the evaluation process.

It is important for prospectus applicants to familiarize themselves with the specific guidelines and instructions provided by Le Rosey School to ensure compliance and a successful application experience.

• Code of Conducts and Ethics

Le Rosey School upholds a Code of Conduct and Ethics that sets clear expectations for student behavior and fosters a positive and respectful learning environment. Here are the highlights of Le Rosey's Code of Conduct and Ethics:

Respect and Integrity: Students are expected to treat all members of the school community, including peers, teachers, staff, and visitors, with respect and dignity. Honesty, integrity, and ethical behavior are core values that underpin all aspects of student life.

Academic Honesty: Le Rosey School places a strong emphasis on academic integrity. Students are expected to complete their assignments, exams, and projects with honesty and without engaging in any form of cheating, plagiarism, or unauthorized assistance. Proper citation and acknowledgement of sources are essential.

Personal Responsibility: Students are encouraged to take responsibility for their actions, choices, and academic progress. This includes attending classes regularly, being prepared for lessons, completing assignments on time, and actively participating in the learning process.

Inclusion and Diversity: Le Rosey School celebrates diversity and promotes inclusivity. Discrimination, harassment, bullying, or any form of intolerance based on race, ethnicity, gender, religion, or any other characteristic is strictly prohibited. Students are expected to foster a welcoming and inclusive environment for all.

Responsible Digital Citizenship: The use of technology and digital platforms is an integral part of modern education. Students are expected to use digital resources responsibly, respecting the privacy and intellectual property rights of others, and adhering to the school's guidelines for online behavior.

Community Engagement: Le Rosey School encourages students to actively engage in the school community and contribute positively to the wider society. Participation in extracurricular activities, service projects, and community events is encouraged, fostering a sense of social responsibility and leadership.

Health and Wellness: Students are expected to prioritize their physical and mental well-being. This includes maintaining a healthy lifestyle, practicing self-care, and seeking support when needed. Le Rosey School provides resources and support services to promote student well-being.

Environmental Stewardship: Le Rosey School promotes environmental awareness and sustainable practices. Students are encouraged to be responsible stewards of the environment, conserving resources, reducing waste, and participating in initiatives that promote sustainability.

Le Rosey School's Code of Conduct and Ethics reflects its commitment to nurturing well-rounded individuals who demonstrate integrity, respect, and a sense of global citizenship. By adhering to these principles, students contribute to a positive and supportive community where learning and personal growth thrive.

Prospective students and their families are encouraged to familiarize themselves with the complete Code of Conduct and Ethics of Le Rosey School to gain a comprehensive understanding of the school's values and expectations.

Le Rosey School upholds high standards of conduct and expects its students to demonstrate integrity, respect, and responsibility at all times. Certain serious offenses may warrant disciplinary action, including suspension.

While the specific policies and procedures may vary, here are some examples of serious offenses that could potentially lead to suspension at Le Rosey School:

Academic Dishonesty: Engaging in acts of plagiarism, cheating on exams, or submitting work that is not one's own can result in disciplinary action, including suspension. Le Rosey School emphasizes academic integrity and expects students to uphold ethical standards in their academic pursuits.

Substance Abuse: Possession, use, or distribution of illegal substances, alcohol, or unauthorized prescription medications on school premises or during school activities is strictly prohibited. Violations of the school's substance abuse policies may result in suspension.

Physical Violence or Threats: Engaging in physical altercations, fights, or acts of aggression towards others, including students, staff, or visitors, is considered a serious offense. Threatening behavior, bullying, or harassment may also lead to suspension.

Theft or Vandalism: Stealing, damaging, or defacing school property, personal belongings of others, or property in the community is a serious violation. Such actions demonstrate a lack of respect for others' rights and may result in disciplinary consequences, including suspension.

Serious Misconduct: Engaging in behavior that poses a significant risk to oneself or others, including acts of endangerment, intimidation, or sexual misconduct, is grounds for disciplinary action, including suspension. Le Rosey School prioritizes the safety and well-being of its students and maintains a zero-tolerance policy for such behavior.

It is important to note that the specific disciplinary procedures and consequences may vary depending on the circumstances, severity of the offense, and the school's policies. Le Rosey School typically follows a fair and transparent disciplinary process that ensures due process and provides opportunities for students to present their perspective.

Prospective students and their families should review the school's code of conduct and disciplinary policies to gain a comprehensive understanding of the expectations and potential consequences for serious offenses at Le Rosey School.

CHAPTER FOUR ☐
School Boards Of Administrations

The Le Rosey School Board of Administration is a group of highly experienced and dedicated individuals who share a deep commitment to providing the best possible education for all students. With a long history of success in providing quality education, the Board of Administration works to ensure that the Le Rosey School's culture of academic excellence is maintained.

As a Board, we are dedicated to providing a safe and nurturing environment for all students, as well as a challenging curriculum to ensure that all students are equipped with the knowledge and skills needed to become successful adults. We are proud of the achievements of our students and strive to provide the highest quality of education to each and every student.

Our goal is to empower our students to reach their fullest potential and to develop their skills for the future.

Brigitte Eugster
French Bilingual Teacher at Richmond and Wandsworth Councils
UCL · Institut Le Rosey

Emilia Sanchez
Chemical Engineer
University of Malaga, Spain · Institut Le Rosey

- ## The Hierarchy Of the Boards Of Administration

Le Rosey School, also known as Institut Le Rosey, is a prestigious Swiss boarding school with a rich history. While specific information about its current board of administration may not be readily available, I can provide a general overview of the hierarchical structure commonly found in educational institutions.

- ## Facts and figures

Board of Trustees: At the highest level, there is typically a Board of Trustees or Board of Governors. This governing body is responsible for overseeing the strategic direction, financial management, and overall governance of the school. The board usually comprises influential individuals such as alumni, parents, business leaders, and educational experts.

Headmaster/Headmistress:
The Headmaster or Headmistress serves as the chief executive officer of the school and is responsible for its day-to-day operations. They work closely with the Board of Trustees, manage the administrative staff, and ensure the effective implementation of educational programs and policies.

Administration: The administrative team consists of various individuals who manage specific areas within the school. This may include positions such as the Director of Finance, Director of Admissions, Director of Academic Affairs, Director of Student Life, and Director of Facilities. Each member of the administration typically oversees their respective department and collaborates with the Headmaster/Headmistress to maintain the smooth functioning of the school.

Faculty: The faculty consists of teachers, instructors, and academic staff who are responsible for delivering the curriculum and providing educational support to the students. They contribute to the development and implementation of the school's academic programs, assess student progress, and engage in professional development activities.

Student Council: In many schools, a student council or representative body exists to give students a voice in decision-making processes and to organize various student activities and events. The student council may have its own hierarchy, including positions such as President, Vice President, Secretary, and Treasurer, among others.

Please note that specific details about Le Rosey's board of administration may have evolved or changed since September 2021. It's always advisable to refer to the school's official website or contact them directly for the most accurate and up-to-date information.

• Qualitative Skills of the Boards Members

The specific requirements for serving on the boards of administration at Le Rosey School may vary, as they depend on the school's governance structure and policies. However, I can provide a general overview of the typical requirements for board members in educational institutions:

• Facts and Figures

Expertise and Experience: Board members are usually expected to have expertise or experience in relevant fields such as education, finance, law, business, or nonprofit management. Their knowledge and skills should align with the needs of the school, allowing them to contribute effectively to the administration and governance.

Commitment and Availability: Serving on a board of administration requires a significant commitment of time and energy. Board members should be willing and able to attend regular meetings, participate in committees, and engage in ongoing discussions and decision-making processes. Availability to respond to urgent matters and emergencies is also important.

Ethical Conduct and Integrity: Board members are expected to uphold high ethical standards and act with integrity. They should be committed to promoting the best interests of the school, making decisions in a transparent and accountable manner, and avoiding conflicts of interest.

Strategic Vision and Leadership: Board members play a strategic role in setting the direction and vision for the school. They should possess strong leadership skills, the ability to think critically and strategically, and a willingness to collaborate with other board members and the administration to achieve the school's goals.

Financial Stewardship: Boards of administration often have a role in overseeing the financial management of the school. Therefore, individuals with financial literacy, budgeting skills, and fundraising experience can bring valuable insights to ensure the school's financial stability and sustainability.

It's important to note that these requirements are general guidelines, and specific requirements for serving on the boards of administration at Le Rosey School may vary. For accurate and detailed information on the specific requirements and processes for board membership, it's recommended to refer to the school's official website or contact them directly.

CHAPTER FIVE □

Students Affairs and Unionism

Welcome to Le Rosey School, where the heartbeat of our institution lies in the dynamic realm of student affairs. We understand that education extends far beyond textbooks and classrooms; it encompasses the holistic growth and development of each individual in our care. At Le Rosey, we strive to create an environment that nurtures the minds, bodies, and spirits of our students, fostering a vibrant community that thrives on diversity, engagement, and collaboration.

Our commitment to student affairs is unwavering. We believe in providing comprehensive support systems that address the unique needs and aspirations of every student. From academic guidance to personal counseling, extracurricular opportunities to social events, our dedicated team of professionals is devoted to ensuring that each student finds their place, explores their passions, and reaches their fullest potential.

Le Rosey School is not just an educational institution; it is a transformative experience. Our student affairs programs are designed to foster a sense of belonging and inclusivity, encouraging students to discover their strengths, challenge their limits, and embrace new perspectives. We cultivate a culture that celebrates individuality while promoting teamwork, empathy, and global citizenship.

In our vibrant and multicultural community, students from diverse backgrounds come together to create a tapestry of experiences, cultures, and ideas. Through a multitude of activities, clubs, and events, students have the opportunity to forge lifelong friendships, develop leadership skills, and broaden their horizons. Le Rosey is a place where students are encouraged to explore their passions, pursue their dreams, and make lasting memories.

As you embark on your educational journey at Le Rosey School, be prepared to be inspired, supported, and empowered. Our student affairs team is dedicated to providing a nurturing environment that promotes academic excellence, personal growth, and well-rounded development. We believe that by investing in the holistic education of our students, we are preparing them to become compassionate, resilient, and innovative global citizens who will shape the world for the better.

Join us at Le Rosey School, where student affairs are at the heart of our mission, and together, we will embark on an extraordinary educational adventure that will last a lifetime.

● Facts and Figures

Le Rosey School is renowned for its exceptional commitment to student affairs, creating a vibrant and inclusive environment that nurtures the holistic development of its students. Here are some facts and figures that highlight the robust student affairs program at Le Rosey:

Diversity and Global Community: Le Rosey School boasts a diverse student body, with students hailing from over 60 different nationalities. This multicultural environment fosters cross-cultural understanding, empathy, and global citizenship among students.

Student Support Services: Le Rosey prioritizes the well-being of its students by providing comprehensive support services. These include academic guidance, counseling, and mentorship programs to address the individual needs of students and support their personal, social, and emotional development.

Extracurricular Activities: Le Rosey offers an extensive range of extracurricular activities and clubs to cater to the diverse interests and talents of its students. These activities encompass sports, arts, music, drama, debate, community service, and more. Students have the opportunity to explore their passions, develop new skills, and engage in teamwork and leadership experiences.

Leadership Development: Le Rosey encourages students to take on leadership roles and actively participate in the decision-making processes of the school. This fosters the development of essential leadership skills, including critical thinking, problem-solving, and effective communication.

Global Experiences and Exchange Programs: Le Rosey School provides opportunities for students to engage in international exchange programs, fostering cultural exchange and global awareness. Students can participate in study abroad programs, international conferences, and cultural immersion experiences, enhancing their understanding of the world and their place in it.

Community Engagement: Le Rosey values community engagement and encourages students to actively contribute to their local and global communities.

Students participate in community service initiatives, volunteer work, and social impact projects, promoting social responsibility and empathy.

Student-Driven Initiatives: Le Rosey believes in empowering students to take ownership of their educational journey. Students are encouraged to propose and lead initiatives such as clubs, events, and projects, fostering a sense of ownership, creativity, and initiative.

These facts and figures underscore Le Rosey School's dedication to student affairs, ensuring that students receive comprehensive support, engage in a diverse range of activities, and develop into well-rounded individuals who are prepared to excel academically and make a positive impact in the world.

STUDENT UNIONISM ☐

Welcome to the vibrant world of unionism at Le Rosey School, where the power of collective action and advocacy ignites positive change. Rooted in a tradition of solidarity and driven by a passion for social justice, our unionism movement stands as a powerful force that empowers students, amplifies their voices, and shapes the very fabric of our school community.

At Le Rosey, we believe that the rights and well-being of students are paramount. Unionism serves as a vital platform for students to come together, express their concerns, and work collaboratively towards solutions. It is a testament to our commitment to fostering a democratic and inclusive environment that values active participation, open dialogue, and equal representation.

Our unionism movement is fueled by a rich history of activism and advocacy. We celebrate the legacy of those who have paved the way for positive change and recognize the power of collective action to address issues and champion causes that matter most to our students. We stand united in the pursuit of social justice, equality, and the advancement of student rights.

Le Rosey's unionism movement is not simply about raising voices; it is about igniting tangible impact. Through organized campaigns, discussions, workshops, and events, we cultivate a culture of civic engagement and empower students to become catalysts for change. We provide a platform for students to address pressing issues, promote inclusivity, tackle discrimination, and create a more equitable and respectful community for all.

Unionism at Le Rosey is not confined to the walls of our school; it extends beyond, connecting us to larger networks and movements regionally, nationally, and globally. By forging alliances and collaborating with other student unions and organizations, we amplify our impact and contribute to the broader fight for social justice and human rights.

As you step into the world of unionism at Le Rosey School, be prepared to be part of a movement that embodies the spirit of empowerment, activism, and solidarity. Together, we will challenge the status quo, break barriers, and shape a better future for ourselves and those around us.

Join us in embracing the power of unionism at Le Rosey School, where students are the architects of change, and together, we will leave an indelible mark on our school, our community, and the world at large.

The following are some general ways in which student unionism can play significant roles in schools:

Advocacy and Representation: Student unions often serve as the voice of the student body, advocating for their rights, concerns, and needs. They represent students' interests in discussions with school administration, participate in decision-making processes, and contribute to the development of policies that affect students.

Community Engagement: Student unions facilitate community engagement by organizing events, campaigns, and initiatives that promote inclusivity, diversity, and social responsibility. They encourage students to actively participate in volunteer work, community service, and social impact projects, fostering a sense of belonging and a commitment to making a positive impact.

Leadership Development: Unionism provides a platform for students to develop leadership skills. By taking on roles within the student union, students gain experience in decision-making, organization, teamwork, and communication. These skills are valuable for their personal growth and future endeavors.

Activism and Social Change: Student unions often engage in activism and social change initiatives, raising awareness about important social issues and advocating for justice and equality. They organize protests, awareness campaigns, and educational events to create dialogue, challenge the status quo, and drive positive change in their school and beyond.

Support and Services: Student unions can play a role in providing support services to students. They may offer resources, guidance, and assistance related to academic concerns, mental health, and general student welfare. They serve as a bridge between students and the school administration, ensuring that students' well-being is a priority.

CONCLUSIONS

In conclusion, the facts and figures about Le Rosey School present a compelling picture of an educational institution that truly stands out from the rest. From its rich history spanning over a century to its stunning location in the Swiss Alps, Le Rosey School encapsulates a unique blend of tradition, excellence, and innovation.

The remarkable student body, hailing from more than 70 countries, fosters a diverse and inclusive environment, enabling students to gain a global perspective and forge lifelong friendships. The school's commitment to academic rigor is evident in its exceptional IB and IGCSE results, as well as its emphasis on holistic education, nurturing students' intellectual, artistic, and athletic talents.

The exceptional faculty at Le Rosey School, comprising passionate educators and renowned experts in their fields, provide students with an unparalleled learning experience. The small class sizes and personalized attention ensure that each student receives the support they need to thrive academically and personally.

Moreover, the school's dedication to innovation and technology integration equips students with the skills and knowledge needed to navigate the challenges of the modern world. The state-of-the-art facilities and extensive extracurricular programs further enrich students' educational journey, enabling them to explore their interests and develop their leadership and teamwork skills.

Beyond the academic realm, Le Rosey School's commitment to sustainability and environmental consciousness sets a powerful example for future generations. The emphasis on responsible citizenship and community service instills in students a sense of social responsibility and empathy, preparing them to become compassionate global citizens and agents of positive change.

In affirmation, Le Rosey School is not just a school; it is an extraordinary institution that empowers students to embrace their full potential and become well-rounded individuals. By combining academic excellence, cultural diversity, and a nurturing environment, Le Rosey School sets the stage for students to embark on a lifelong journey of growth, discovery, and success.